THE **I** FACTOR

HOW TO **I**NFLUENCE YOUR WORLD

ACTION WORKBOOK
BY JIM EGLI AND BEN HOERR

THE I FACTOR: HOW TO INFLUENCE YOUR WORLD

Published by TOUCH Outreach Ministries, Inc.
P.O. Box 19888
Houston, TX 77224-9888 USA
(281) 497-7901 • Fax (281) 497-0904

©Copyright 1993 by *North Star Strategies*
1500 N. Lincoln Avenue
Urbana, IL 61801
(217) 384-3077

Printed in the United States of America

This **Action Workbook** is designed for Small Group members seeking to influence their world with the love of Jesus. There is also a leader's packet available that contains a Leader's Guide and other helpful tools. For more help related to Small Group (Cell) Church strategy, contact TOUCH Outreach Ministries or *North Star Strategies* at the addresses above.

ACTION WORKBOOK | CONTENTS

PREFACE

"Me . . . an evangelist? Oh, that's not my gift, and besides, there are others who can do a much better job than I, like Scott, Rita, . . ."

While it is true that not every Christian is called to the office of evangelist, God desires each one of us to influence our world (see Mt.5:13-16; 28:18-20). The question is, "How can I positively influence my world for Christ and His Kingdom?" That's what this book is all about -- **Influencing Your World**. In case you have not figured it out yet, the "I" stands for "Influence." Through this *Action Workbook*, you will be equipped through very simple, direct, and practical steps to cooperate with the Holy Spirit in positively influencing the lost in your world.

ACKNOWLEDGMENTS

Thanks to our wives, Vicki and Tina, for their constant encouragement and support. You gals are fantastic! Also a big "thank you" to Carol Goelitz for meticulously typing this book and seeing it through its improvements and revisions. We appreciate you, Carol.

COME, FOLLOW ME, AND
I WILL MAKE YOU FISHERS OF MEN.

- Jesus

Jesus issues a call. Do you hear it? A call to companionship, obedience, adventure. Our job is simply to come and follow. For us, as for those who first heard these words, it might mean leaving some things behind -- dropping some tasks at hand, shifting priorities, or releasing misconceptions.

The making job, however, is His. He is not asking you to make yourself into something, but just to walk with Him, allowing Him to graciously work in and through you.

Also, be encouraged! We are in this together. The fishing James and John did was with nets, not poles. It took teamwork; so does influencing others with Christ's love. Jesus is working in us and through us *together*.

Listen again. Do you hear Jesus' call? Are you coming?

INSTRUCTIONS

This *Action Workbook* consists of six one-hour lessons. Your Small Group will work through one lesson per week. Each lesson begins with a SHARE time where we discuss how we did on our weekly assignments. The LEARN section is a training time led by the Small Group Leader where we study the Bible, answer questions, discuss issues in small groups, role-play, and practice. The DO section contains several practical assignments to be completed by each member in the week following. Each lesson concludes with a time to MINISTER to one another as the Holy Spirit directs.

SHARE

Until now, you may never have heard of the word *oikos*. However, this Greek word found in the Bible will become a very important part of your vocabulary as you reach out to your lost friends. As an introduction to understanding *oikos*, let's reflect on some of your thoughts towards evangelism and how you were influenced to receive Christ. Take five minutes to answer the questions below, and then break up into small groups of 2-3 and share your responses to questions 3-5.

1. What pictures or images come to your mind when you hear the word "evangelism"?

2. Why do you think many Christians feel inadequate and fearful about evangelism?

3. Who was most influential in your decision to follow Christ? What was that person's relationship to you (friend, teacher, parent, etc.)?

4. What did that person *do* which influenced you?

5. Describe how that person made you *feel*.

6. What did that person *say* which influenced you?

 **LEARN**

WHO INFLUENCES WHOM TOWARD CHRIST?

The Church Growth Institute has done a variety of surveys asking over 14,000 lay persons, "What or who was responsible for your coming to Christ and the church?" The percentage of responses have been:

A special need	1-2%
Walk in	2-3%
Pastor	5-6%
Visitation	1-2%
Sunday school	4-5%
Evangelistic crusade	0.5%
Church program	2-3%
A friend or relative	75-90%

These statistics reveal what you probably have seen in your own life and in the lives of those close to you. That is, **the great majority of people who come to Christ are brought by ordinary people -- friends, neighbors, co-workers, and relatives -- who take a genuine interest in them, serve them, share their lives, and eventually share the Gospel.** This is the most natural and effective method of "evangelism."

STEP 1 | IDENTIFY YOUR *OIKOS*

UNDERSTAND THE *OIKOS* PRINCIPLE

Scripture reveals the same truth that we see in research and in personal experience. The word *oikos* in the New Testament refers to a person's "household," their extended network of relationships. Repeatedly in the Gospels and in the Book of Acts, we see people influencing those in their *oikos* to Christ.

1. Who became Christians along with Lydia (Acts 16:15)?

2. Who followed the Philippian jailer in receiving Christ (Acts 16:31-33)?

3. Who heard the Good News of Christ with Cornelius (Acts 10:1-2, 22-24)?

4. Who did Matthew invite to his home to meet Jesus (Matthew 9:10)?

5. What do these illustrations teach you about using your relationships as bridges to influence others and share Christ's love?

(For further study, other examples of the *oikos* principle can be seen in Luke 8:38-39 / John 1:40-41, 44-45; 4:49-53 / Acts 18:7-8.)

STEP 1 | IDENTIFY YOUR *OIKOS*

IDENTIFY YOUR *OIKOS*

Every human being in every social structure actually lives in a special, tiny world known as their *oikos*. While we may know hundreds of people, we have a very few close, meaningful relationships. This small group of family, relatives, neighbors, and work/class mates is our *oikos* -- our personal community.

God's plan is that we influence the members of our *oikos* who do not know Him. Through serving them in love, helping meet their needs, and sharing our lives together, we may see them become open to the Gospel. But this all starts by simply building meaningful personal relationships with them. Could you identify the members of your *oikos* which you think are yet unreached by the Gospel?

1. Relatives - people related to you by blood or marriage
   a.
   b.
   c.
   d.

2. Friends - people you share activities with or enjoy being with
   a.
   b.
   c.
   d.

3. Neighbors - people who live nearby
   a.
   b.
   c.
   d.

4. Workmates/Classmates - people you see regularly at work or school
   a.
   b.
   c.
   d.

STEP **1** | IDENTIFY YOUR *OIKOS*

 DO

Are you willing to let Christ make His love real to your *oikos* through you? Are you willing to pray daily for their salvation?

Turn to the *Oikos* **Prayer Checklist** on page 40. In the blanks provided, write the names of 4-8 *oikos* members. Use the checklist provided there to pray daily for these individuals.

The concept of the "Listening Room" means taking special time each day to just listen to God. As you come to God daily in prayer, spend time in the "Listening Room." Listen to Him and His ways as He calls you to pray, build relationships, and serve the lost in your *oikos*. The key to a successful "Listening Room" experience is that you stop, ask the Lord to speak, and listen. Use the space below to record your "Listening Room" instructions about your *oikos*.

 **MINISTER**

Invite the Holy Spirit to come and minister to each individual as He desires.

STEP **2** | COOPERATE WITH GOD

SHARE

Last week our assignment was to begin praying daily for the unsaved members of our *oikos*. How did you do? What did you hear in the "Listening Room"? (Have each group member take a turn to briefly share.)

LEARN
JESUS' WORD PICTURE FOR EVANGELISM

Break up into groups of 2 or 3 to answer the following questions. Report your findings to the group.

1. Jesus repeatedly used the same word picture for evangelism or influencing others to Him. What basic image does Jesus use in Mark 4:2-8?

2. What does this parable suggest to you about influencing others?

3. How does the Apostle Paul describe our role and God's role in evangelism (I Cor.3:6-8)?

Now only God can make seeds grow. In this sense, we are not responsible for the size of the harvest, or how many people ultimately receive Jesus Christ. But every believer is to faithfully obey God's call to cultivate, plant, and water the seeds -- that is, cooperate with the Holy Spirit by building relationships, sharing God's truth, and serving the lost.

STEP 2 | COOPERATE WITH GOD

UNDERSTAND THE PROCESS OF EVANGELISM

In the book *Power Evangelism,* John Wimber and Kevin Springer illustrate the process of evangelism using the Norton-Engel scale. Our objective is to meet people where they are and cooperate with God to move them up the scale.

SPIRITUAL DECISION PROCESS
MAN'S RESPONSE

•	Effective sharing of faith and life
•	Openness to others
•	Prayer
•	Stewardship of resources
•	Christian life-style
•	Discovery and use of gifts
•	Growth in Christian character
•	Growth in understanding of the faith
+3	Begin making other disciples
+2	Initiation into the church
+1	Evaluation of decision

A NEW DISCIPLE IS BORN (Mt.28:19-20)

-1	Repentance and faith
-2	Challenge and decision to act
-3	Awareness of personal need
-4	Positive attitude to the Gospel
-5	Grasp of implications of the Gospel
-6	Awareness of basic facts of the Gospel
-7	Interest in Christianity
-8	Initial awareness of Christianity
-9	No effective knowledge of Christianity
-10	Awareness of the supernatural

The supernatural experience of salvation cannot be explained by a chart. God works however He chooses, as is demonstrated by the lack of a set pattern of salvation in the Bible. While this scale is not the final word, it does illustrate a general process that allows you to identify where people are and how you can cooperate with God in reaching them.

STEP 2 | COOPERATE WITH GOD

COOPERATE WITH THE SPIRIT

Different factors impact people and lead them toward Christ. Some people's journey is more of an intellectual one. This intellectual quest for truth about God, life, and the Bible often requires the longest time period. A second factor influencing people to Christ is signs and wonders. When people experience Christ's healing touch, a direct answer to prayer, or the release of spiritual gifts through believers, their journey toward Christ is rapidly accelerated. They may be "propelled" through several stages of receptivity in one moment! A third factor is the drawing power of vital, meaningful relationships with believers. A fourth factor is change in human predicament. (More on this in a moment.)

Often all of these factors are intertwined. The important thing to realize is that by **being sensitive to the Holy Spirit**, timely ministry to people's real needs can manifest God's concern and power in a way that deeply speaks to them.

1. After Jesus had risen from the dead, He described His followers' basic job assignment to them five different times (Mt.28:18-20/ Mk.16:15-20/Lk.24:45-49/Jn.20:21-22/Acts 1:8). On how many of these occasions did He promise the presence of the Holy Spirit?

2. In John 14:11-12, what does Jesus promise us about ministering in the power of the Spirit?

3. In John 16:7-9, whose job does Jesus say it is to bring conviction to unbelievers?

4. To what does Jesus attribute His success according to John 5:19?

When we reach out to unbelievers, we make an exciting discovery: The Holy Spirit has often gotten there ahead of us and is working in their lives and preparing their hearts. God deeply loves each person and is seeking them out. It is our privilege to cooperate with Him in making Christ's love real.

BE AWARE OF PERIODS OF RECEPTIVITY

As mentioned above, a person's openness to spiritual things is often effected by recent life experiences or changes in the human predicament. Factors impacting individual's lives are listed below. As you read through these factors, place the initials of unsaved *oikos* members next to experiences they have encountered in the past year.

_____ Death of a spouse
_____ Divorce
_____ Marital separation
_____ Jail term
_____ Death of a close family member
_____ Personal injury or illness
_____ Recently married
_____ Fired from work
_____ Marital reconciliation
_____ Retirement
_____ Change in family member's health
_____ Pregnancy
_____ New family member
_____ Business readjustment
_____ Change in financial status
_____ Death of close friend
_____ Foreclosure of mortgage or loan
_____ Change in work responsibilities
_____ Son or daughter leaves home
_____ Outstanding personal achievement
_____ Spouse starts work
_____ Start or finish school
_____ Change in living conditions
_____ Revision of personal habits
_____ Change in working conditions
_____ Change in residence
_____ Change of schools

STEP 2 | COOPERATE WITH GOD

DO

1. Continue to pray daily for those on your *oikos* list. Ask the Holy Spirit to be at work in their hearts. Pray that God will use you and other Christians to reveal His love to them. Check off the days on your ***Oikos* Prayer Checklist**. Record your "Listening Room" instructions here:

2. Do one activity to expand your *oikos*; that is, establish a new relationship or build a friendship with someone you only know casually now.

3. Do one activity to serve an *oikos* member right now in a time of crisis or need. (See the receptivity chart on the previous page to identify a person.) Record who and what below:

MINISTER

1. What two members of your *oikos* would you like your Small Group members to be praying for?

_____   _____

2. Write the names of those shared by your Small Group members on the back inside cover of this workbook.

STEP 3 | LOVE OTHERS TO CHRIST

 **SHARE**

Last week our Assignment was to continue praying daily for the unsaved members of your *oikos* and to do one activity to extend your *oikos*. How did you do? What did you hear in the "Listening Room"? (Have each group member take a turn to briefly share.)

 **LEARN**

FOLLOW CHRIST IN LOVING OTHERS

**People don't care how much we know
until they know how much we care.**

Let's look at several Scriptures that give us some insight about building relationships and loving others to Christ.

1. What do the Pharisees' words in Luke 15:2 tell us about Jesus' attitudes and actions toward "sinners"?

2. How did Jesus describe His ministry to a lost world (Mk.10:45)? What does this say about our lifestyle and outreach to unbelievers?

3. Read Matthew 5:14-16. What do you think Jesus meant? How will unbelievers be drawn to God the Father?

STEP 3 | LOVE OTHERS TO CHRIST

LOVE BY LISTENING

What do Proverbs 18:13 and James 1:19 teach us about reaching out to unbelievers?

One of the most powerful ways to express love to unbelievers is to genuinely listen to them. If unbelievers sense that we want to quickly fix their problems, dispense advice, stuff the Bible down their throat, or that they are our "evangelism project," they are apt to get angry or defensive. On the other hand, as we listen with non-judgemental acceptance, we show respect for who they are and what they think, feel, and believe. Over time, a bridge of trust is built that allows them to share their heart and reveal their needs and spiritual openness. At some point, we may be privileged to cross that bridge and share the Gospel!

Here are a few practical active listening skills:
- Give full attention to the person talking. Don't be thinking about what you're going to say when the other person stops talking.
- Reflect what you are hearing
  - "Let me see if I understand you correctly . . ."
  - "Am I correct in saying . . ."
  - "So the major concern you have right now is . . ."
  - "I thought I heard you say . . ."
  - "You are feeling _____ because _____ . . ."
  - "You seem to be feeling (thinking) . . ."
  - "It appears . . ."
  - "Are you saying . . ."
- Don't interrupt, butt in, or complete someone's sentences
- Ask for clarification of details when necessary, but discipline your curiosity
- Maintain good eye contact

LOVE BY ASKING QUESTIONS

Sometimes asking questions can express sensitivity and genuine concern. This is especially the case when you have a growing relationship with the person already. We don't want to be perceived as Sergeant Friday conducting an interrogative interview. However, a few well-chosen questions can be a non-threatening way to initiate spiritual conversation, help us connect with people at the appropriate place in their spiritual journey, and help us gauge where the Holy Spirit is already working in their life. The Norton-Engle scale (pg.12) can help us determine what type of questions would be appropriate for them.

Below we have listed some questions from different sources that we have found helpful.

1. Waldron & Scott's questions
    a. John, are you interested in spiritual things?
    b. Have you ever thought about becoming a real Christian?
    c. If someone were to ask you, "What is a real Christian?", how would you answer?

2. Paul Little's questions
    a. Have you ever personally trusted Christ or are you still on the way?
    b. How far along the way are you?
    c. Would you like to become a Christian now?

3. George Hunter's questions
    a. Where has God helped you in the past?
    b. What experiences in life have you had where you were helped to get through something and felt that Someone was guiding you?

STEP 3 | LOVE OTHERS TO CHRIST

    c.   Has God proven that He is worthy of your more complete trust?

    d.   Do you desire to open your whole life to Him?

4.   Other questions

    a.   When have you felt God's closeness or help in your life?

    b.   If you could ask God for anything right now, what would it be?

    c.   Where are you at in your relationship with Christ today?

    d.   Where are you on your spiritual journey?

    e.   Are you ready to give your life to Christ now?

    f.   How do you feel about . . . (God, life after death, the church, your early childhood religious training, etc.?)

    g.   Do you believe in God? If you do, what is the nature of your relationship with Him?

    h.   What hinders you from personally trusting in Jesus?

    i.   Why don't you go to church?

    j.   If you could design the ideal church, what would it look like?

    k.   If you could ask God one question, what would it be?

Timing is important whether you are harvesting fruit or reaping souls. If you pick something off the tree too soon, it may never ripen. On the other hand, if you don't pick it when it is ripe, it will spoil and go to waste. As Jesus did, we can use questions to uncover felt needs and to gauge people's spiritual openness.

LOVE BY SERVING

Another way we can love unbelievers to Christ is by building friendships and serving them. Listed below are a few activities that we can use to develop relationships and meet needs.

Building Friendship

Share a dinner together

Throw a block party

Play cards

Attend a Tupperware party

Play miniature golf

Go shopping together

Have a progressive dinner

Go on a picnic or have a cookout

Pop some corn and watch a video

Celebrate anniversaries, birthdays

Go bowling

Play racquetball, tennis, golf, basketball, volleyball

Have a neighborhood game night in your home

Have a party (4th of July, Memorial Day, New Year's Eve)

Serving In Love

Babysit for free

Rake and bag leaves

Chaperone a school dance

Coach a little league team

Help with outdoor projects

Mechanical advice

Visit the hospitalized

Shovel snow

Serve in PTA or be a room mother

Organize school car pool

Offer your area of expertise

Conduct an investigative Bible study

Look after widows or single moms

Deliver candy or cookies at Christmas

Pet-sit or house-sit during vacation

Send get-well, birthday, or anniversary cards

Take a meal, pie, or cookies to new neighbors

Provide a dinner in the event of family illness or death

Mow lawn, especially while neighbors are on vacation

STEP 3 | LOVE OTHERS TO CHRIST

DO

1. What two members of your *oikos* did you ask your Small Group members to be praying for last week?

   _____   _____

2. What special thing can you do in the week ahead to serve each of these persons and express concern to them?

3. Continue to pray daily for all of those on your *oikos* list, checking off the days as you pray.

4. Spend time in the Listening Room. What insight is God giving you for how to pray or how to serve? Is God showing you a new way He wants you to expand your *oikos* through serving? This week write down one or two things you think the Holy Spirit is saying.

5. Extra credit: Gauge someone's spiritual openness this week by asking, "Are you very interested in spiritual things?" If they say "no," drop the subject. If they say "yes," ask them where they are on their spiritual journey.

MINISTER

Invite the Holy Spirit to come and minister to each individual as He desires.

STEP 4 | SHARE YOUR STORY

 **SHARE**

Report to one another how your assignments from last week went. Are you consistently praying? What do you hear God saying in the "Listening Room"? What actions have you completed?

 **LEARN**

HEARING AND RESPONDING

Not many of us responded to the Gospel the very first time we heard it. Most of us needed to hear it again and again. It took time to consider the claims of Christ and what receiving Him would really involve for us. Just like any other major decision in life, it took a while to weigh our options, count the cost, and make our decision.

As we reach out to pre-Christians, we should keep this in mind. Although a few people respond enthusiastically to the Gospel the first time they hear it, for most people it takes time and multiple exposures to the message. Consider the rich variety of ways that you can expose friends to the good news of Christ:

- Share your testimony
- Conduct an Investigative Bible study
- Attend a Christmas service or a Christian concert
- Give them a New Testament or a relevant book
- Suggest listening to a good radio preacher
- Bring them to a Sunday Celebration
- Serve them in some practical, meaningful way

What are some other ways you could expose your friends to the Gospel?

THE POWER OF PERSONAL TESTIMONY

One of the most meaningful ways for people to hear the good news of Christ is through your personal testimony. Here are some of the reasons why sharing your personal experience of Christ opens people's hearts and minds to consider what He can do for them:

- It is personal and from your heart
- You have credibility with your audience
- No one can deny its reality
- It is a non-threatening way to share the reality of Christ, His love, and His power
- It includes testimony to what God is doing today
- It can be adapted to speak to the felt needs of individuals

ARE YOU READY?

As we witness to Christ's presence in our lives, it is helpful to remember our role. The witness in a court room is not responsible to convince the jury. His or her role is to testify to what he or she has experienced. The verdict or decision is not in their hands. In the same way, when we give a "testimony" to Christ's work in our lives, it is our privilege and responsibility to simply relate what Christ has done for us.

Look at I Peter 3:15 and Colossians 4:5-6. What instructions do these Scriptures give us to guide our personal sharing?

STEP 4 | SHARE YOUR STORY

GET READY

Paul's testimony in Acts 26:9-23 gives us a helpful pattern for organizing our own story. This is the "**BEST**" testimony outline. It contains these elements:

B -- Before you were saved
E -- Events leading up to salvation
S -- Salvation day
T -- Today

Now you will prepare a brief personal testimony by following the instructions below and writing key phrases in the outline provided. This will prepare you to share your story when the occasion is appropriate.

Some people's testimony cannot follow the **BEST** outline because they received Christ early in life. They are like Timothy who apparently received Christ at a very young age (see II Timothy 3:14-15). If you have a "Timothy" testimony, skip point **B** and **E** below and begin with **S**. If you confidently know Christ as Savior and Lord but can't remember when or how you received Him, write down under **S** what it means to have Christ as Savior and Lord of your life and what it means for someone to accept Him.

(B) <u>**Before You Were Saved**</u>
What were key factors in your life before Christ?
- Build bridges and establish common ground with your listener.
- Don't use disgusting details or glory in past sins.

STEP **4** | SHARE YOUR STORY

Ⓔ **Events Leading Up To Salvation**

What events and circumstances led up to your receiving Christ?

- Use one key principle or problem (lack of peace, pride, lack of direction, emptiness, etc.).
- How did this effect your day-to-day life?
- Share fears and thoughts.
- Share something good about your life before Christ so others can relate to you (morality, generosity).

Ⓢ **Salvation Day**

How did you receive Christ, and what difference did it make in your life?

- Focus on Christ -- His love and His provision.
- What thoughts were going through your mind?
- How did it happen?
- Specifically tell people how you received Christ so that when they want to make a commitment they will know what to do.
- Emphasize one Scripture.
- Avoid religious jargon; use words they can easily understand.

STEP 4 | SHARE YOUR STORY

(T) **Today**

How did Christ change your life, and how is He at work now?
- Show how Christ dealt with fears, problems, etc. from the principles mentioned previously.
- Focus on the most striking change.
- Be honest -- Christ has come into your life, but He still has some work to do.
- Share about peace, confidence, and assurance of salvation.
- Share your excitement for what Christ is doing in your life now.

DO

1. Memorize I Peter 3:15.

    "But in your hearts, set apart Christ as Lord. Always be prepared to give an answer to everyone who asks you to give the reason for the hope that you have. But do this with gentleness and respect." (NIV)

2. Continue to pray daily for those on your *oikos* list. As you pray daily, consistently take time in the "Listening Room" to hear God's voice. What do you hear God saying?

3. Engage in one activity to expand your *oikos*; that is, to make new friendships or to begin significantly deepening a casual friendship. Write the activity below.

4. Complete a serving activity to express God's love in a new way to someone in your *oikos*. Indicate your activity here.

5. Extra credit: Gauge someone's spiritual openness this week by asking, "Are you very interested in spiritual things?" If they say "no," drop the subject. If they say "yes," ask them where they are on their spiritual journey.

 **MINISTER**

Invite God to grant you confidence and joy in sharing with others what He has done for you. Minister to one another as the Holy Spirit directs.

STEP 5 | SHARE HIS STORY

SHARE

Review the memory verse from last week's assignment. Do you have it memorized?

> I Peter 3:15 "But in your hearts, set apart Christ as Lord. Always be prepared to give an answer to everyone who asks you to give the reason for the hope that you have. But do this with gentleness and respect." (NIV)

Report to one another how your assignments from last week went. Are you continuing to pray daily for your *oikos*? What did you hear in the "Listening Room"? What did you do in the past week to build relationship with and serve unbelievers?

LEARN

SHARING THE GOOD NEWS OF CHRIST

As we have seen over the last four weeks, evangelism is much more a process of loving people to Christ than presenting a canned speech of the Gospel facts. (Remember how many of our negative preconceptions about evangelism had to do with uncaring "Jesus sales people"?) By building meaningful relationships with unbelievers and serving them in love, bridges of mutual trust are built. As we stay sensitive to the Holy Spirit, listening to His instructions and doing what He prompts us to do, we will find the hearts of our *oikos* opening to the Gospel. In fact, there will probably come a time when they welcome our clear presentation of the Gospel. Each Christian should be prepared to share the five essential truths of salvation for the times God opens the door of receptivity in our lost friends.

LEARN THE 5 ESSENTIAL GOSPEL TRUTHS

Sharing the truths of the Gospel -- God's love for people, our basic sinfulness, Jesus' death and resurrection, the need to trust Christ, and God's desire for a lifelong, personal relationship -- can be done in a *variety* of ways. It may take five minutes or five months or five years. We may share these truths one at a time or all at once. However it's done, we need two things: firstly, utter dependence upon the Holy Spirit, and secondly, a thorough understanding of these Gospel truths.

Many believers have found it helpful to have a "model" Gospel presentation to draw upon as the need and Holy Spirit dictate. This simple tool captures the essential truths by focusing upon five key words:

- **God**
- **Sin**
- **Jesus Christ**
- **Receive**
- **Relationship**

This adaptable presentation contains three aspects: key words, Scriptures, and a simple diagram. You will not necessarily use all three elements every time, but we recommend that you know all three so that you are prepared to share in the best way in any given situation.

STEP 5 | SHARE HIS STORY

REVIEW THE GOSPEL CONTENT

In the explanation below, we have included one key Scripture verse for each truth and a simple diagram for those inclined to share pictorially.

1. **GOD loves you and wants a relationship with you.**

   John 3:16 "For God so loved the world that he gave his one and only Son, that whoever believes in him shall not perish but have eternal life."

2. **Your SIN keeps you from God.**

   Romans 3:23 "For all have sinned and fall short of the glory of God."

3. **JESUS CHRIST died and rose again to forgive your sin.**
   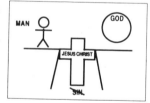
   I Peter 3:18 "For Christ died for sins once for all, the righteous for the unrighteous, to bring you to God."

4. **You must RECEIVE Jesus as your Lord and Savior.**
   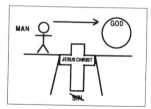
   John 1:12 "Yet to all who received him, to those who believed in his Name, he gave the right to become children of God."

5. **Your trust in Jesus Christ begins a lifelong RELATIONSHIP.**
   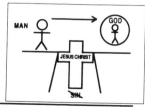
   John 15:5 "I am the vine; you are the branches. If a man remains in me and I in him, he will bear much fruit; apart from me you can do nothing."

STEP 5 | SHARE HIS STORY

REMEMBER THESE SIMPLE GUIDELINES

1. Have an attitude of complete dependence on God as you share.

2. Remember that only the Spirit of God can convict someone of their need for salvation in Christ. Let your prayer and your speech reflect this fact.

3. Ask questions and listen carefully to be sure that each point is understood. Always respect the other person's opinion.

4. If someone asks a tough question, don't be afraid to reply, "I don't know, but I'll see if I can find an answer."

5. Be sensitive to the person's reaction. Gauge your response and continued sharing accordingly.

Person's Reaction	Your Response
Eager and positive	Invite the person to receive Christ by praying with you, or on their own at a later time
Seriously considering, but not ready to pray	Ask the person to think about what you have discussed and then talk to him/her later. Consider inviting them to an evangelistic Bible study
Skeptical or negative	Maintain politeness or warmth, leaving a positive impression

PRACTICE SHARING HIS STORY

A friend has just asked you to explain how to become a Christian. Draw and explain the content of the Gospel below:

STEP 5 | SHARE HIS STORY

 DO

1. Continue to pray for the unbelievers on your *oikos* list, inviting God to make His love real to them through you and other Christians. Consistently take time in the "Listening Room" to hear God's voice and instructions to you.

2. Memorize the references that go with the simple Gospel presentation.

3. Do at least one activity to serve unbelievers, expressing Christ's love to them.

4. Complete an activity to expand your *oikos* or an activity to introduce unbelievers in your *oikos* to Christian friends.

 **MINISTER**

Minister to one another as the Holy Spirit directs.

STEP 6 | REACH OUT TOGETHER

SHARE

How are you doing on your weekly assignment? Are you praying consistently for those on your *oikos* list? What are you hearing God say as you take time in the "Listening Room"? What experiences are you having as you reach out to build relationships and serve unbelievers?

After you have shared as a group your responses to the questions above, take several minutes to review the Scripture verses used with the Gospel truths which we learned last week. Write the appropriate reference beside each key word:

- **God:**
- **Sin:**
- **Jesus Christ:**
- **Receive:**
- **Relationship:**

LEARN

UNDERSTAND THE NEED FOR TEAMWORK

What do John 4:36-38 and I Corinthians 3:6-8 teach us about the need for teamwork in evangelism? How might this work in the context of your Small Group?

COOPERATE WITH YOUR TEAMMATES

What does Jesus say will be one of our most powerful and convincing "witnessing tools"? (See John 13:34-35)

When we introduce unbelieving friends to Christian brothers and sisters, they get a more complete picture of Christ. None of us individually are able to adequately reflect His love.

Write the name of someone from your *oikos* list below:

_____

Write down several ways that you might introduce this person to other members of your Small Group or other Christian friends.

Write the name of someone else from your *oikos* list below:

_____

What are some ways you might introduce this person to Small Group members or other Christian friends?

STEP 6 | REACH OUT TOGETHER

CREATE OUTREACH OPPORTUNITIES

One exciting way to reach out as a Small Group is through special activities that you plan together. A Social Night about every six weeks provides your Small Group a great opportunity to build relationships and have fun. Whether you have a picnic, go bowling, or play cards, these are all excellent times to invite unbelieving friends, spouses, neighbors, or family members. This provides an opportunity to build relationship with them, introduce them to Christian friends, and acquaint them with your Small Group.

Sometimes the activity you choose can be specifically geared toward the *oikos* members of your Small Group. Thinking of your *oikos* members, what social activity could your group plan that might interest and appeal to them?

PRAY TOGETHER

Many of the prayers in the New Testament focus on outreach. The early believers prayed together for evangelism and requested prayer from one another in their outreach efforts (Mt.9:37-38 / Eph.6:19-20). Read Acts 4:29-30. What specific things did the early church pray for in this passage?

What prayer does Paul request in Colossians 4:3-4?

Where do *you* need prayer as you seek to follow Christ in loving others to Him?

Are you as a Small Group willing to commit to pray consistently for those in each other's *oikoses*? How? When?

STEP **6** | REACH OUT TOGETHER

GIVE BIRTH TO NEW GROUPS

The early church in the first century primarily met in homes (Rom.16:5 / I Cor.16:19 / Philemon 1:2). As more people became Christians and the church grew, new meetings were begun in other homes. This is the same way the Small Group Church grows today. Beginning new groups opens up fresh opportunities for outreach and ministry.

However, when the number of people in a group exceeds 10, its effectiveness is diminished. This is because opportunities for meaningful discussion, sharing, and ministry decrease as the number of people grows. People (especially the quieter and more reserved) begin to feel left out and conclude that their contribution is unimportant. So, we really need to keep a Small Group small! The only way to do this as we include new people is to birth new groups.

There are two ways to begin a new group. One way is to "multiply" your group. When a group multiplies, two new groups are formed with roughly an equal number of people in each group. A second way to start a new group is to "launch" one. When a new group is launched, the core of the existing group remains the same, but a handful of people are blessed and released to begin a new group.

"Giving birth" is a traumatic yet joyful experience! When a new baby is brought into the world, it requires pain and travail; yet it results in joy and celebration. The same thing is true when new groups are birthed. It's not easy to go through the "labor" of transition. Yet the results are well worth the effort. Perhaps the hardest part is the separation of relationships which appears to take place. That's why when groups multiply, we encourage them to occasionally meet together for social activities.

When might your group be ready to give birth through multiplication or launching a new group?

<table>
<tr><td>**STEP 6**</td><td># REACH OUT TOGETHER</td></tr>
</table>

 DO

1. What do you want to do as a group in the months ahead to support one another in personal outreach? Talk about it now.

2. In what ways do you want to reach out together through social activities or special events? Discuss it.

3. Are you open and praying for new people to join your group? Are you thinking about when you might want to multiply or launch a new group? Continue to pray about this personally and as a group.

4. Continue to pray daily for *oikos* members.

5. Complete an activity this week to introduce an *oikos* member to a Christian friend or family.

 **MINISTER**

Minister to one another as the Holy Spirit directs.

DAILY *OIKOS* PRAYER LIST

1. _____   5. _____
2. _____   6. _____
3. _____   7. _____
4. _____   8. _____

The chart below is to help you in the venture of praying daily for your *oikos*. As you pray each day, check off the appropriate day on this chart.
- Invite God to continue His work in each life.
- Ask Him to make His love real to each of these persons *through you*.
- Pray for His Kingdom to come in their life.
- Ask God to meet their needs.
- Seek gifts of the Holy Spirit for them.

With pencil, darken daily as you pray.

	1	2	3	4	5	6	7	8	9	10	11	12	13	14	15	16	17	18	19	20	21	22	23	24	25	26	27	28	29	30	31
Jan																															
Feb																													■		
Mar																															
Apr																															■
May																															
Jun																															■
Jul																															
Aug																															
Sep																															■
Oct																															
Nov																															■
Dec																															

SMALL GROUP *OIKOS* PRAYER LIST

This section is to be completed with Step 2. On the inside of the back cover, make a prayer list from the *oikos* members of your Small Group. Pray weekly for these people.